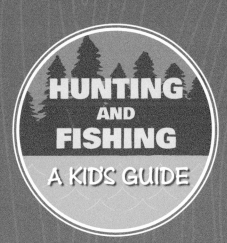

HUNTING AND FISHING
A KID'S GUIDE

We're Going
FRESHWATER FISHING

Andrea Palmer

PowerKiDS press.

New York

Published in 2017 by The Rosen Publishing Group, Inc.
29 East 21st Street, New York, NY 10010

First Edition

Editor: Melissa Raé Shofner
Book Design: Tanya Dellaccio

Photo Credits: Cover John Kuczala/Getty Images; back cover, pp. 1, 3, 4, 6, 8–10, 12, 14–16, 18–20, 22, 24, 26–28, 30–32 ArtBitz/Shutterstock.com; all pages except p. 2 sittipong/Shutterstock.com; p. 5 John McCormick/Shutterstock.com; p. 7 Matt Jeppson/Shutterstock.com; p. 9 (top) Sekar B/Shutterstock.com; p. 9 (bottom) IDAK/Shutterstock.com; p. 10 Ljupco Smokovski/Shutterstock.com; p. 11 Olga Visavi/Shutterstock.com; p. 13 Dewitt/Shutterstock.com; p. 15 (top) Krzysztof Odziomek/Shutterstock.com; p. 15 (bottom) francesco de marco/Shutterstock.com; p. 17 Steve Chenn/Getty Images; p. 19 (top) Hero Images/Getty Images; p. 19 (bottom) Joel Sartore/Getty Images; p. 21 Pavel Bybko/Shutterstock.com; p. 23 WOLF AVNI/Shutterstock.com; p. 24 Hans Christiansson/Shutterstock.com; p. 25 goodluz/Shutterstock.com; p. 27 (top) Don Mammoser/Shutterstock.com; p. 27 (bottom) David Ryznar/Shutterstock.com; p. 29 Isantilli/Shutterstock.com; p. 30 IrinaK/Shutterstock.com.

Cataloging-in-Publication Data

Names: Palmer, Andrea.
Title: We're going freshwater fishing / Andrea Palmer.
Description: New York : PowerKids Press, 2017. | Series: Hunting and fishing: a kid's guide | Includes index.
Identifiers: ISBN 9781499427493 (pbk.) | ISBN 9781499428728 (library bound) | ISBN 9781508152811 (6 pack)
Subjects: LCSH: Fishing–Juvenile literature. | Freshwater fishes–Juvenile literature.
Classification: LCC SH445.P35 2017 | DDC 799.1'1–dc23

Manufactured in the United States of America

CPSIA Compliance Information: Batch Batch #BW17PK: For Further Information contact Rosen Publishing, New York, New York at 1-800-237-9932

CONTENTS

A NOTE TO READERS

Always talk with a parent or teacher before proceeding with any of the activities found in this book. Some activities require adult supervision.

A NOTE TO PARENTS AND TEACHERS

This book was written to be informative and entertaining. Some of the activities in this book require adult supervision. Please talk with your child or student before allowing them to proceed with any hunting activities. The author and publisher specifically disclaim any liability for injury or damages that may result from use of information in this book.

FRESHWATER FUN

Fishing is a popular sport around the world. People of all ages love to go fishing in ponds, lakes, rivers, and streams. These tend to be bodies of freshwater. Freshwater is water that has almost no salt in it.

You can catch freshwater fish in pretty much any body of water that is not the ocean. Freshwater fishing is the most common kind of fishing in the United States. This is because many Americans live near bodies of freshwater.

HUNTING HINT

Some of Earth's lakes are salty, but most have freshwater.

Lake Superior is the largest freshwater lake in the United States. Many people enjoy fishing for trout and salmon there.

LIVING IN FRESHWATER

Scientists believe there are more than 30,000 species of fish on Earth. A species is a group of plants or animals that are the same kind. Nearly 60 percent of all fish are saltwater species. Saltwater fish live in the ocean.

Less than half of all fish are freshwater species. Perch, bass, catfish, pike, walleye, and trout are some of the more common types of freshwater fish found in the United States.

HUNTING HINT

Most fish are covered in scales. Their scales are often coated with **slime** to help them move through the water.

This is a rainbow trout. There are many types of trout in the United States. The most common are rainbow, brown, and brook trout.

FISH ON THE MOVE

Several kinds of fish live in freshwater some of the time and salt water some of the time. For example, some salmon are born in freshwater, but **migrate** through streams to the ocean when they grow older. After a few years, these salmon return to freshwater to spawn, or lay their eggs. Salmon found in **landlocked** bodies of water live in freshwater all the time.

One kind of trout, called a steelhead, also migrates from salt water to freshwater. After spawning, steelhead return to the ocean. They can make several migrations in their lifetime.

Salmon need to be strong swimmers. They swim upstream, against the flow of the river, to lay their eggs.

HUNTING HINT

Some steelhead trout migrate in the warmer summer months, while others migrate during the colder winter months. This makes for good fishing all year long.

GRAB YOUR GEAR

You'll need a lot of gear if you want to go fishing. Fishing gear is also called tackle. Tackle includes things such as hooks, lures, bait, rods, and reels. A reel holds your fishing line.

There are several kinds of rods and reels people use when freshwater fishing. One kind of rod is an ultralight fishing rod. This type of rod is good for catching small fish. It's shorter and weighs less than most other rods do. It also bends more.

HUNTING HINT

Some people like to stand in the water while they fish. They often wear tall boots or special pants, called **waders**, to keep them warm and dry.

These fishing rods have lures on them. Lures are things used to draw in and catch fish. They come in many colors and often look like bugs or small fish.

11

USING BAIT AND LURES

Fisherman use bait, or things that fish like to eat, to draw fish to them. Sometimes they use lures instead of bait. The kind of bait or lure that works best depends on what kind of fish you want to catch.

In order to catch a fish, you need a lure or a hook with bait on it at the end of your line. After baiting your line, cast it by swinging your rod out over the water. Then sit back and wait for a fish to bite.

HUNTING HINT

Freshwater fish like to eat worms, **leeches**, crawfish, crickets, grasshoppers, and small fish called minnows. These creatures all make great bait.

This bass was caught using a fishing lure. You can see the brightly colored lure hanging out of the fish's mouth.

FINDING FISH

Two of the best places to find fish are where they hide and where they eat. Fish like to hide in places that keep them out of the current, or fast-moving water. They also like to hide where above-water predators, such as bears or birds, can't easily see them.

Places where one stream flows into another are often good **sources** of food for fish. Fish also feed where rivers and streams bend. These places make good fishing spots.

Be careful where you cast your fishing line. You may end up catching underwater plants or branches instead of a fish.

HUNTING HINT

Sometimes lakes and ponds are stocked with fish. This means fish have been added to the water so there will be plenty for people to catch.

ON LAND OR BY BOAT?

Many times people fish from land, but sometimes they fish from a boat. Fishing from land can save you time and money. However, you may have fewer places to find fish.

Without a boat, you'll need to stay along the shore or in **shallow** streams. One of the hardest parts of fishing in streams and rivers is that the water is often moving quickly. If you're not careful, you could lose your footing in the current.

HUNTING HINT

Children can often fish without a fishing **license**. Check your state's wildlife department website for the rules in your area.

Fishing from a dock will put you farther out on the water than if you fished from the shore. Don't fish from a dock unless you have **permission** from the owner.

17

BOATING SAFETY

A boat will help you reach a lot of great fishing spots. There are many different kinds of boats. **Canoes** and rowboats are quiet, but they're slow and you need to paddle them. Motorboats have engines, which makes them faster but also loud. No matter what kind of boat you have, make sure it's in good shape.

Make sure you have a plan for where you're going. It's also important to be aware of the weather and the location of other boats. You don't want to crash your boat.

HUNTING HINT

You should always wear a life jacket when fishing from a boat. This is important even if you know how to swim. You should also never go fishing alone.

Small boats are great for fishing in ponds. Bigger boats work best in lakes or large rivers.

canoe

FIRST FISHING TRIP

A lake or a pond is a great place for your first fishing trip. There are lots of plants there for fish to eat and hide under. Logs, rocks, and docks provide places for fish to find shade from the sun and to hide from bigger fish that want to eat them.

You can fish in a lake or a pond from the shore or from a boat. Places that are deeper or shallower than the areas around them are good spots to look for fish.

HUNTING HINT

Worms can be used as bait when you go freshwater fishing. You can dig them up yourself or buy them from a bait shop.

Lily pads and other plants make great hiding places for fish. Try casting your line nearby, but be careful it doesn't get tangled.

FLY-FISHING

Fly-fishing is a type of freshwater fishing. It's harder than other types of fishing. A fly-fisher uses special lures and a different kind of cast. If you want to go fly-fishing, you'll need a fly-fishing rod and reel.

A common way to cast your line in fly-fishing is called the overhead cast. To do this cast, you gently snap your line backward and forward over your shoulder in a smooth movement. Your fishing line should stay above the water so it doesn't become tangled.

HUNTING HINT

If you know an adult who enjoys fly-fishing, don't be afraid to ask them for tips.

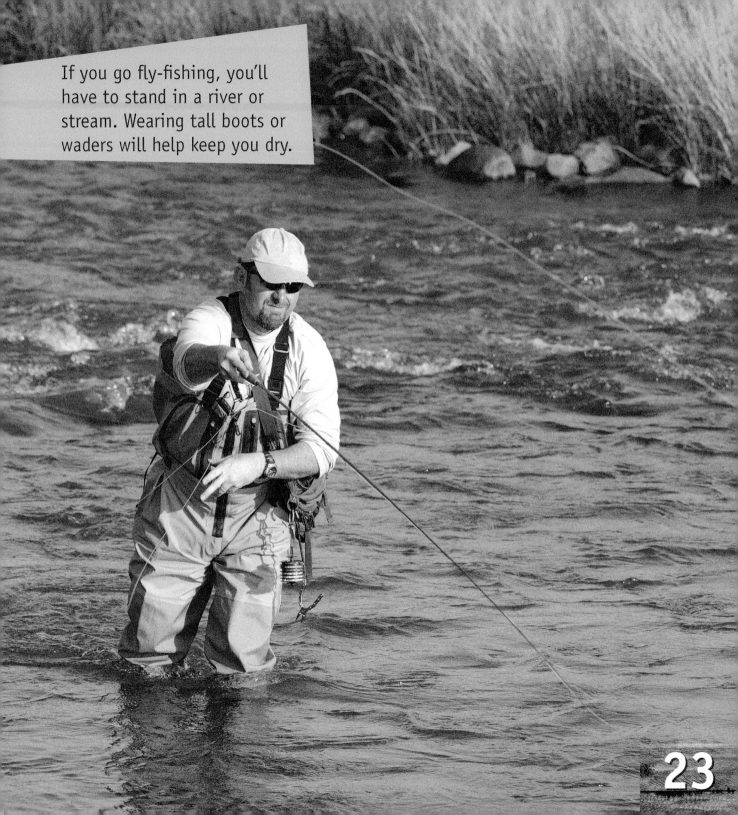

If you go fly-fishing, you'll have to stand in a river or stream. Wearing tall boots or waders will help keep you dry.

23

Special fly-fishing lures are made out of hair, string, feathers, and other things. They're called flies because many are made to look like insects, or bugs. Some flies today are made to look like other creatures that fish like to eat. Fly-fishing lures are perfect for tricking hungry fish.

Different flies are made for catching different kinds of fish. Some lures are made to "swim" through the water. Others are made to fly though the air. People have been tying flies for centuries. It's both a science and an art.

dry-fly
fishing lure

It's a good idea to bring a net with you when you go fishing. It will help you bring in your catch.

HUNTING HINT

Dry-fly fishing is a type of fly-fishing where the fly never goes below the surface of the water. It takes a lot of practice!

25

GIGGING AND NOODLING

Gigging is a type of fishing in which you **spear** fish. It's a very old form of fishing that was used by Native Americans. Today, gigging is a popular sport in the Ozark Mountains.

Noodling is another fishing method that was first used by Native Americans. Noodlers hunt for catfish with their hands instead of a fishing rod. Noodling is fun, but it can also be unsafe. Very large catfish can pull noodlers underwater. It's against the law in some states because of this.

HUNTING HINT

Noodlers should be strong swimmers since they spend so much time in the water.

gigging

In Missouri, gigging season runs from mid-September through the end of January. A season is the period of time when you're allowed to catch certain types of fish or use certain fishing methods.

noodling

Noodlers use sticks to poke around underwater inside logs, under rocks, and in mud banks to find catfish. For safety reasons, you should never go noodling alone.

AFTER THE CATCH

Catching your first fish is a special moment. If your fish is large enough, you may be able to keep it and eat it. An adult can help you remove the scales and bones and cook your catch.

You can also use the catch-and-release method of fishing. This means you remove the hook from the fish's mouth and then carefully put the fish back in the water. Be sure to hold the fish gently when you're letting it go. The catch-and-release method lets more people enjoy fishing.

HUNTING HINT

Check to see if your state has a bag limit before going fishing. A bag limit is the highest number of fish that you're allowed to catch and bring home.

Many people go fishing while on a camping trip. Fish can be caught and released or cooked over the campfire.

EARTH-FRIENDLY FISHING

It's important to clean up any trash from your fishing trip. Be sure to pick up your extra line. Fishing line can easily get tangled around the legs of birds and other animals. Never leave a baited hook anywhere. A bird could eat it by mistake and choke.

Also, don't be too noisy during your fishing trip. If you run around, shout, or play a radio loudly, it will bother those around you, including the fish. A fishing trip is a great way to connect with nature. Enjoy it, but be respectful.

HUNTING HINT

When you catch your first fish, you may want to ask someone to take a picture of you holding it!

GLOSSARY

canoe: A light, narrow boat that is pointed at both ends and that is moved through the water by paddling.

landlocked: Surrounded by land.

leech: A type of worm that lives in the water and sucks the blood of animals.

license: An official paper giving someone the right to do something.

migrate: To move from one place to another.

permission: The right or ability to do something that is given by someone who has the power to decide if it will be allowed.

shallow: Not deep.

slime: A thick, slippery liquid.

source: A person, place, or thing from which something comes or where it can be found.

spear: A long pole with a sharp point at one end.

waders: High waterproof boots or pants worn for walking or standing in deep water, especially while fishing.

INDEX

WEBSITES

Due to the changing nature of Internet links, PowerKids Press has developed an online list of websites related to the subject of this book. This site is updated regularly. Please use this link to access the list: www.powerkidslinks.com/hunt/fresh